This book belongs to

. . . .

First published 2021 by Bark Wrinkle Books, Sherborne, Dorset, UK.

This edition published 2024

Copyright © 2021 Richard Jansen

All rights reserved. No part of this publication may be reproduced, distributed, or transmitted in any form or by any means, including photocopying, recording, or other electronic or mechanical methods, without the prior written permission of the publisher, except in the case of brief quotations embodied in critical reviews and certain other noncommercial uses permitted by copyright law.

ISBN: 978-1-7391582-0-0

Bear Foot

Written and illustrated by

Richard Jansen

Humphrey wandered through the wood,
Further than a bear cub should.

Searching for berries for his tea,
He saw something shiny by a tree.

FLY, ZOOM, BOOST and AIR.

He slipped them on, "Gosh they're comfy!"
Then skipped home, a happy Humphrey.

"I found them there, beyond the hill. They'll help me run, I'm sure they will."

Humphrey wore the shiny shoes,
Until one day he could not move.

He fell while running down a track.
"Ouch!" he cried, "I've hurt my back."

He tried a hop and a skip.
"Ouch!" he cried, "I've hurt my hip."

He tripped and crashed into a tree,
"Ouch!" he cried, "I've hurt my knee."

Taking off a shoe, he saw
A bright red, painful, shoe-shaped paw!

"Without these shoes, my paws were stronger.
I will not wear them any longer."

His bear cub pals were all confused.
"Why leave the shiny shoes unused?"

"They weren't so great, I was misled.
I couldn't feel the ground," he said.

Humphrey spread his claws and smiled.
Without the shoes, he could rewild!

Bounding barefoot through the trees,
Back to his best, he was so pleased.

"GRROOOAHHH!" he roared, on all fours,
Feeling the dirt between his claws.

WHOOSH! He sped through the sand,
Knowing where his paws should land.

CRUNCH!
He trod on twigs and sticks.

Without the shoes, his paws were fixed.

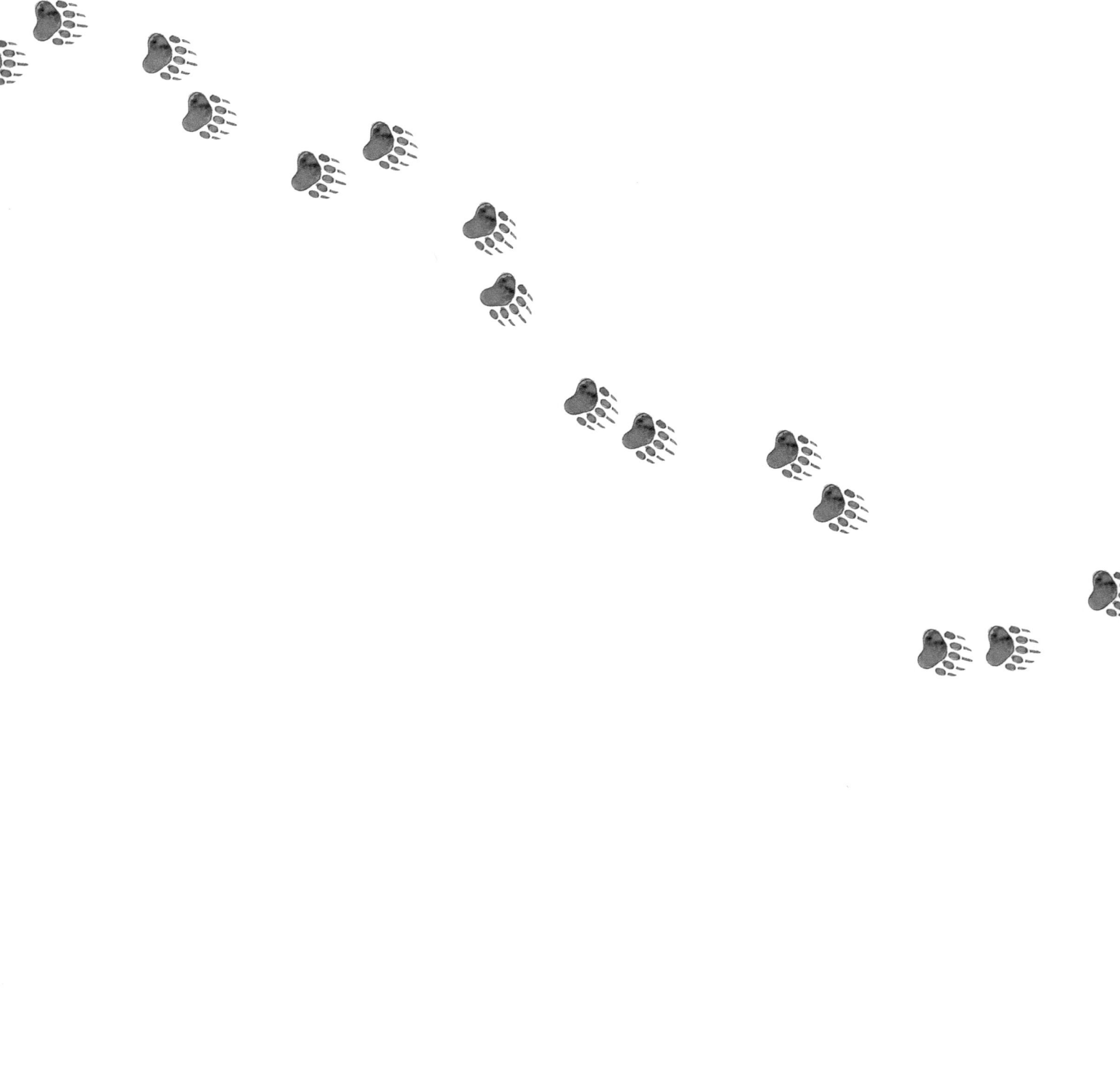

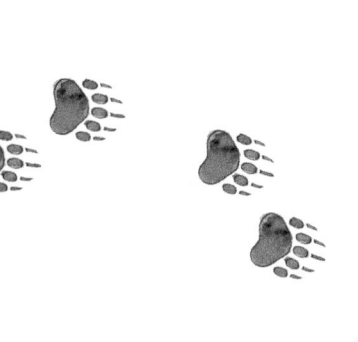
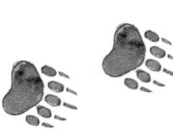
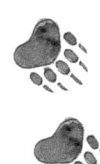

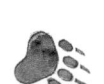

Richard Jansen

is a physiotherapist and dad of two from Somerset in the UK. Richard's love of running (sometimes barefoot!) was the inspiration to write Bear Foot.

@bearfootchildrensbook